THE
GUITAR
FINGER**GYM**

Build Stamina, Coordination, Dexterity and Speed on the Guitar

SIMON**PRATT**

FUNDAMENTAL**CHANGES**

The Guitar Finger Gym

Build Stamina, Coordination, Dexterity and Speed on the Guitar

Published by **www.fundamental-changes.com**

ISBN: 978-1-78933-054-0

www.fundamental-changes.com

Twitter: **@guitar_joseph**

Over 10,000 fans on Facebook: **FundamentalChangesInGuitar**

Instagram: **FundamentalChanges**

For over 250 Free Guitar Lessons with Videos Check Out

www.fundamental-changes.com

Cover Image Copyright ShutterStock: ktsdesign / SemiSatch

Contents

Get the Audio

The audio files for this book are available to download for free from www.fundamental-changes.com and the link is in the top right corner of the site. Simply select this book title from the drop-down menu and follow the instructions to get the audio.

We recommend that you download the files directly to your computer, not to your tablet, and extract them there before adding them to your media library. You can then put them on your tablet, iPod or burn them to CD. There is a help PDF on the download page, and we provide technical support via the contact form.

Kindle / eReaders

To get the most out of this book, remember that you can double tap any image to enlarge it. Turn off 'column viewing' and hold your kindle in landscape mode.

Twitter: **@guitar_joseph**

Over 10,000 fans on Facebook: **FundamentalChangesInGuitar**

Instagram: **FundamentalChanges**

For over 250 Free Guitar Lessons with Videos Check Out

www.fundamental-changes.com

Introduction

People visit the gym to heighten fitness, increase stamina, build endurance and improve their overall performance. In this book you will visit the guitar finger-gym where you will train your fingers to achieve new levels of dexterity, stamina, and coordination.

The exercises featured in this book suit both electric and acoustic guitar. Whether you are a beginner, intermediate, or an advanced player, anyone can benefit from the examples featured in this book. Although there is no easy way to hone your technique, the examples given here will provide shortcuts and will produce massive results in your guitar playing.

The exercises I have provided are adaptable, so feel free to change any of the strategies and techniques to suit your specific guitar requirements. For beginners, I recommend starting at the first chapter and working your way through the book from start to finish. More advanced players can pick specific exercises and techniques they focus on areas they are struggling with and dedicate their practice time to mastering those examples.

The examples featured throughout this book are laid out in a logical fashion and can be worked on as a long series of exercises or as individual ideas. It is far better to exercise for a few minutes every day, rather than for thirty minutes once a week.

At the end of the book, I have provided sample guitar finger-gym 'workouts'. These workouts are divided up into 10 minute, 15 minute, 30 minute and 60 minute sessions. They will help you create a balanced practice routine that combines all the elements in each chapter.

The majority of book contains small bite-size examples that develop specific areas of your guitar playing but the final chapter includes a track I wrote called Dexterous Driver. Each workout will end by playing this track so you can always finish your practice routine with a full piece of music.

The audio for this book is available from **http://www.fundamental-changes.com/download-audio** so you can hear how I play and *phrase* each example. The backing tracks provide a perfect platform for you to explore each lick and technique.

All the examples in this book will improve your guitar technique but remember that the most fundamental principle is to always enjoy yourself and have fun playing music.

Happy Playing!

Simon

Chapter One - Dexterity and Coordination

During my playing career I've noticed that on certain days, I can play at the top of my ability fairly quickly, but on other days, it takes much longer than I anticipated to feel comfortable and creative. The days I play my best are the ones where I had properly warmed up all areas of my playing.

This chapter focuses on how to improve your dexterity and coordination, and this will warm your fingers up extremely quickly.

Consider these key points when learning the following examples.

1) Ensure there is *space* between the fingers of your fretting hand. By learning to play these examples with room between your fingers, you will develop strength in the correct tendons and muscles of the hand.

2) Keep your knuckles upright at all times.

3) Try to always keep each finger in one designated fret (the one-finger-per-fret).

4) Aim for minimal movement in your fretting and picking hands.

5) Stop if you feel any pain. When it comes to guitar playing, 'no pain no gain' is never the way forward. Stretch thoroughly before you play the examples in this chapter and stop if you feel any strain.

One Finger Per Fret

Stick to the *one-finger-per-fret* rule when learning these examples unless otherwise stated. The idea behind the rule is that you allocate one finger to each fret that you play. For example, if you play notes between the 1st and 4th frets, use your first finger for the 1st frets notes, your second finger for all 2nd frets notes, etc. This can be seen in the diagram below:

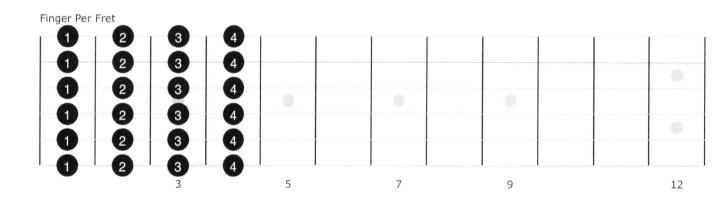

Using A Metronome

When you are developing your technique using these finger-gym examples try to always use a metronome.

Begin playing each example very slowly with the metronome set at 50bpm, and make sure that every note is clean and audible. Watch your picking hand and notice if you are applying the strict 'down, up' alternate picking pattern required.

When you can play an example perfectly three times in a row at 50bpm, try raising the metronome up to 53bpm. Continue to increase the metronome speed in increments of 3 beats-per-minute up to your target speed of 80bpm+.

This form of structured practice means that you will only increase your speed once the lick is played accurately.

I use the Tempo app (made by Frozen Ape) on my phone, as I know I will always have my phone with me, then I never have an excuse practice without a metronome.

The first example is a popular guitar warm-up. Start off at 50bpm and make sure that each pick stroke is clean and perfectly in time. (there should be four notes per click). Use alternate picking (down up down up) throughout this example.

Example 1a

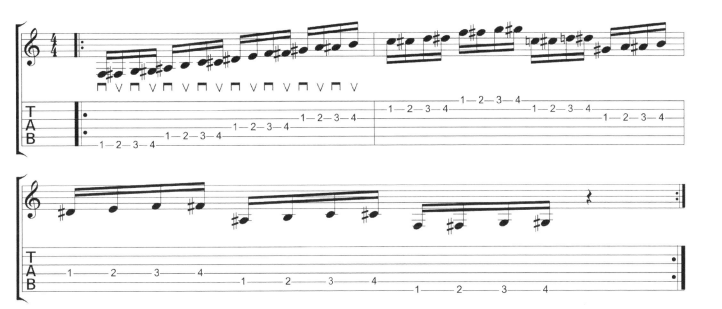

Example 1b is the reverse of example 1a. Starting on your fourth finger can feel a little trickier than beginning on your first finger but with regular training, all your fingers will feel equally dexterous.

Example 1b

Example 1c is the pattern I often play as my first warm when picking up my guitar. It uses the ascending pattern seen in example 1a, and descends with example 1b but played one fret higher. If you only have time for one example from this chapter I highly recommend this one.

Example 1c

I first started dedicating time to working on my coordination and dexterity after watching videos of Joe Satriani warming up. Example 1d is a pattern he often uses when preparing for a session or to play live.

Example 1d – Satriani-style Warm Up 1

Example 1e is the reverse of the pattern in example 1d. Once again start off slowly with a metronome and only speed up the metronome once you can play the pattern three times correctly in a row.

Example 1e – Satriani-style Warm Up 2

In example 1f I combine the pattern in example 1d with the pattern in 1e. This is a useful dexterity and coordination builder.

Example 1f – Satriani-style Combination 1

Reversing example 1f gives us another challenging Satriani-style dexterity warm-up.

Example 1g – Satriani-style combination 2

Example 1h uses the first finger as a pedal note. The goal is to keep each note as even and clean as possible. For a tougher challenge try using hammer-ons and pull-offs.

Example 1h – Pedal note

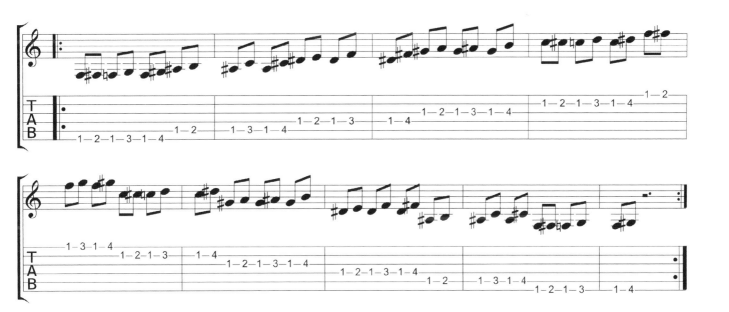

Here is an adaption of the original '1234' exercise from example 1a. In this example, stretch out your fourth finger to play the 5th frets on each string. Don't overdo this exercise, especially if you are not used to this type of stretching.

Example 1i – 1234 Stretching

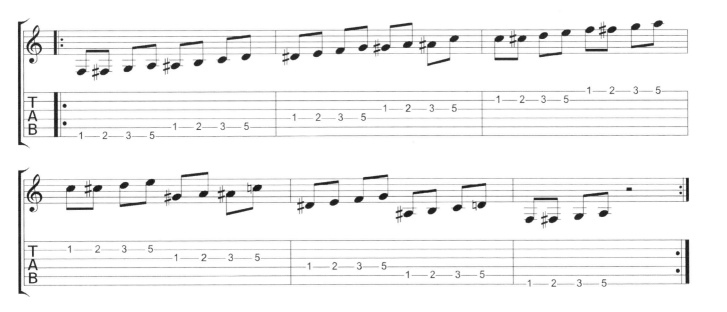

Instead of playing frets '1234' sequentially, example 1j introduces a string skip between each note.

Example 1j – Cross String 1234

Example 1k adds interest to your dexterity warm-ups by using larger string skips. Keep using the one-finger-per-fret method.

Example 1k – String Skipping

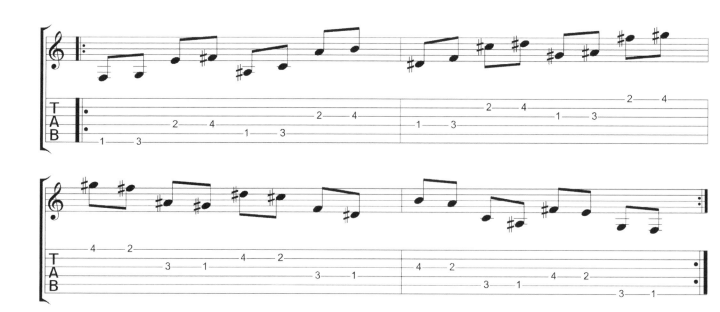

Finger Agility

Normally, the third and fourth fingers will require more development than the first and second fingers. The next two help you to achieve independence between fingers three and four. In example 1l, hold down the 1st and 2nd frets with your first and second fingers but don't play the notes. Then using only your third finger, complete the second bar without moving your first and second fingers.

Example 1l – Third Finger Agility

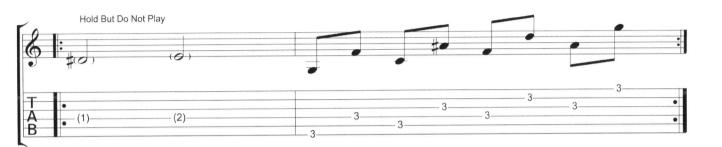

Example 1m follows on from example 1l but works on the fourth finger independence. Hold down the 1st, 2nd, and 3rd frets with your first, second, and third fingers but don't play the notes. Then play the second bar using only your fourth finger, aiming not to move the original three fingers.

Example 1m – Fourth Finger Agility

Dexterity Conclusion

In this chapter, I have shown you a wide range of exercises that will improve dexterity in all your fingers. From finger independence to stretching exercises, this chapter forms the foundation of all the following exercises. Think of dexterity developing the body's core muscles in your guitar finger-gym workouts.

The examples shown in this chapter can be challenging and it is important not to overwork your hands. If you feel any pain after playing the examples, stop and take a break before returning to the exercises. Taking regular breaks and even rest days can help prevent injuries.

Most players will never encounter a problem when working on the examples in this chapter, but do make sure you stretch thoroughly and don't overdo it.

I use the Egoscue method daily as a form of gentle stretching. It has helped keep my hands, arms and shoulders flexible despite endless hours of guitar playing.

Chapter Two – Strength and Control

Strength and control are often overlooked when improving technique. Learning to build both of these qualities will help you play at your best for longer periods of time.

In the previous chapter, we used alternate picking (down up) on every example. In this chapter we will use hammer-ons and pull-offs to develop control with different finger combinations. In exactly the same way as before, use the one-finger-per-fret rule (unless otherwise stated) and a metronome when practicing.

An important concern when playing legato (using hammer-ons and pull-offs) is to *keep each note the same volume*. This means that the picked note and the legato notes that follow should all have very similar dynamics. Try recording yourself playing the following examples and pay attention to how smooth the transition is between the picked and legato notes.

This chapter is divided between hammer-ons and pull-offs to help you focus on developing the strength and stamina needed to complete each example for an extended length of time.

Hammer-ons

To execute a hammer-on, play a note and then quickly 'hammer' a different finger onto a higher fret. The result is two notes from just one pick stroke.

Begin slowly and use the practice regimes at the end of the book to help you organise the material in this chapter.

Example 2a uses the first and second fingers to play the 1st and 2nd frets, and uses a hammer-on between the notes.

Example 2a

In this example we hammer-on from the 1st to the 3rd frets using the first and third fingers.

Example 2b

The next stamina exercise hammers the 1st fret to the 4th fret and uses the first and fourth fingers.

Example 2c

Examples 2a to 2c used the first finger to start each hammer-on. The next examples use the second finger and will build strength and control in different finger groupings. Example 2d uses the second and third fingers to hammer-on the 2nd fret to the 3rd fret.

Example 2d

In the next example, hammer from the 2nd fret to the 4th fret on each string. Use your second and fourth fingers.

Example 2e

Now we move into building strength and endurance using the third and fourth fingers. Example 2f may require more work than the previous examples, but start off slowly at around 50bpm and only build up speed when you feel comfortable.

Example 2f

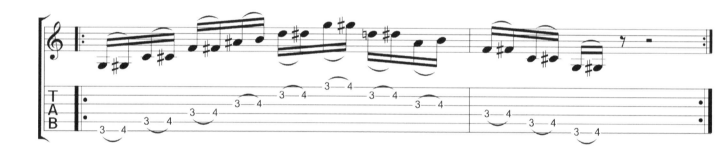

In example 2g I have created a hammer-on warm up for each finger. The first and second fingers will likely feel the strongest here, so you may find that your third and fourth finger require more practice to get the hammer-ons to sound clean. Use a down pick before every hammer-on on each string.

Example 2g

Pull-Offs

Now we have learnt some useful hammer-on patterns to build strength and control, it is time to learn the reverse and develop pull-off strength in all fingers. A pull-off is the reverse of a hammer-on. Begin by picking a fretted note and then pull your finger off the string (downwards towards the floor) to sound a fretted note below the first.

In example 2h you are going to pull-off from the 2nd fret to the 1st fret on each string. Make sure you start each string by fretting the 2nd fret with your second finger before pulling that note off to the 1st fret on your first finger.

Example 2h

In the next example, pull-off from the 3rd fret to the 1st fret using your third and first fingers.

Example 2i

The next exercise is to pull-off from the 4th fret to the 1st fret. Pick the 4th fret with your fourth finger fretting that note and pull-off to the 1st fret on your first finger.

Example 2j

Repeat every example in this chapter with both a metronome and a timer you will gain confidence to play for longer periods of time.

Use a simple timer, like a stopwatch, to time your practice. Record how long you can play each exercise for every day and try to beat that time when you next practice.

In example 2k use your third and second fingers to pull-off between the 3rd and 2nd frets.

Example 2k

The next stamina exercise pulls off the 4th fret to the 2nd fret and uses the fourth and second fingers.

Example 2l

The final individual pull-off example uses the fourth and third fingers to pull-off from the 4th fret to the 3rd fret.

Example 2m

Example 2n

Example 2n is the reverse of example 2g. This time, we are using pull-offs on every string instead of hammer-ons.

Combining Hammer-Ons and Pull-Offs

When you have worked on hammer-ons and pull-offs as separate exercises you can build patterns that use a combination of the two. The following three examples show some classic strength-builders that will help you to play for longer periods of time and will work on your legato control.

Example 2o combines a pull-off from the 2nd to the 1st fret with a hammer-on to the 3rd fret. Like all the examples in this book, use the one-finger-per-fret pattern to complete each exercise.

Example 2o

The next idea uses a '214' grouping of notes, once again combining a pull-off with a hammer-on.

Example 2p

For the final control-building exercises use a '324' note grouping. Create your own legato-based stamina exercises based on these examples.

Example 2q

Stamina Conclusion

Building strength and control is an on-going process. Little by little you will be able to play for longer periods of time without becoming fatigued. Although each example in this chapter is just a few bars long, the idea is to repeat them without stopping for as long as possible.

Pick an example from this chapter and put on a stopwatch to see how long you can play it consistently without getting tired. Keep track in a guitar journal of how long you were able to play it for, and each day try to beat that previous time.

As with all the chapters in this book don't push yourself too hard. Instead of pushing through any pain or tiredness, take regular breaks, stretch and relax between all the examples.

1.

Chapter Three – Endurance and Stamina

Backing Track One – A Major

Now that you have worked on your dexterity and your stamina, it is time to put your endurance to the test. This is one part of guitar technique that is often overlooked, but it will begin to enable you to play at your peak level for longer periods of time. That will mean that when you are playing live, or even just jamming with a backing track you won't run out of steam. I have purposefully made the A Major Backing Track five minutes long. Try to play over the whole thing continuously without stopping when working on an example in this chapter.

As with any exercise demonstrated in this book, be sure to watch out for any soreness or pain and make sure to take regular breaks when needed. Building endurance happens gradually but allows you to play for long periods without feeling tired or sore!

In the following examples we will be using the A Major scale in position 1 but you should also try the exercises with other scales that you know. As you learn new scale shapes, I recommend referring back to this chapter to build endurance with them. In the appendix I have included some common scale shapes in full neck diagram form.

For more details on scales check out **Guitar Scales in Context** by Joseph Alexander.

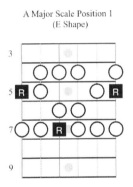

A Major Scale Position 1
(E Shape)

Example 3a is shows simple, but highly effective concept for building endurance. In this example, play the A Major scale continuously until you are too tired to carry on. Use a stopwatch and note down how long you lasted, and next time you practice try to beat that time.

Example 3a – Continuous A Major Scale

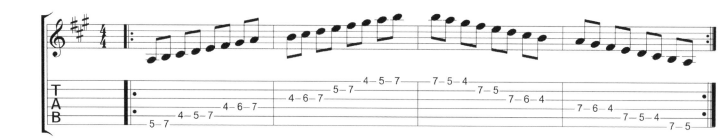

Using scale sequences can help build endurance and break up longer scale shapes into more manageable chunks. Example 3b uses notes from the A Major scale on the D and G strings and repeats them in a cyclic fashion. Alternate pick this pattern, or for more of a challenge, can add hammer-ons and pull-offs to create legato phrasing.

Example 3b – Repeating A Major Pattern 1

Example 3c creates a similar patter to example 3b but uses the G and B strings exclusively.

Example 3c – Repeating A Major Pattern 2

The next example uses an A Major scale pattern on the B on E strings. Loop each sequence with a metronome until your hands start to feel slightly fatigued.

Example 3d - Repeating A Major Pattern 3

Example 3e uses a descending A Major scale pattern on the A and D strings.

Example 3e - Repeating A Major Pattern 4

In the following example, use a descending A Major scale pattern on the D and G strings. For an added challenge add hammer-ons and pull-offs.

Example 3f - Repeating A Major Pattern 5

Example 3g uses the same pattern as seen in the previous examples but on the B and E strings.

Example 3g - Repeating A Major Pattern 6

Example 3h combines multiple shapes of the A Major scale and uses slides to connect the notes. The full A Major scale neck diagram is shown below.

Example 3h – Continuous Scales with Slides

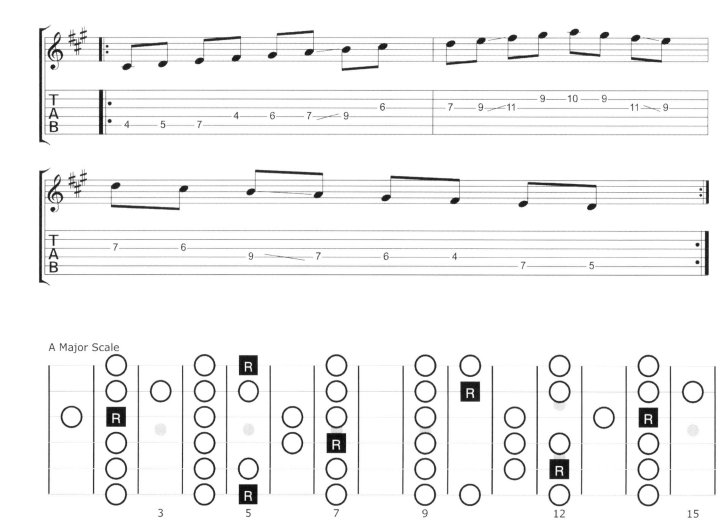

A Major Scale

Mini Lick Builders

Examples 3i to 3n act as both endurance exercises and mini licks in the key of A Major. Play Backing Track One and loop each example for as long as you can before your hands start to tire. Write down how long you were able to last, and gradually extend your total duration each day.

Example 3i uses a repeating hammer-on pattern on the B and the E strings.

Example 3i

Example 3j uses pull-offs on the B and E string. You may find you tire more quickly using pull-offs than hammer-ons. This is natural at first, but with regular practice, all your legato patterns will become equally comfortable.

Example 3j

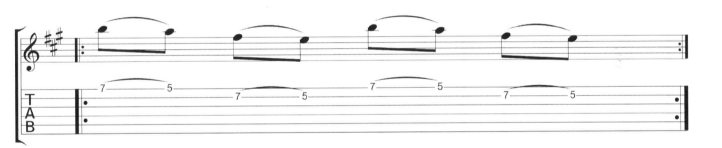

Example 3k introduces a hammer-on pattern with a wide stretch. Use your fourth finger to play the 9th fret on the E string.

Example 3k

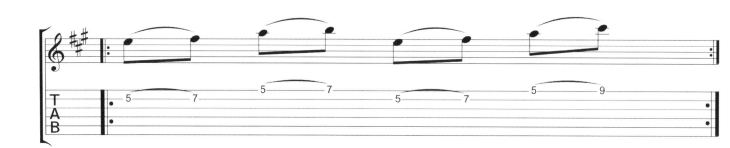

The next example reverses the previous idea to create a challenging pull-off pattern. As always, start off extremely slow at around 50/60bpm and make sure you can play each example three times correctly with a metronome before raising the tempo.

Example 3l

Example 3m demonstrates a two-bar hammer-on sequence that uses multiple positions of the A Major scale on the top two strings. Backing Track One works wonderfully as an accompaniment to these examples.

Example 3m

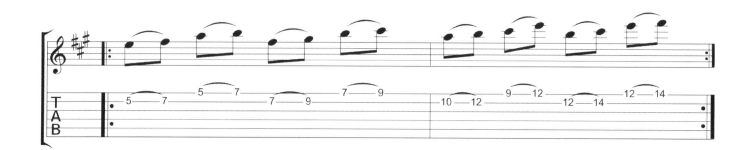

This example uses a pull-off pattern to descend the A Major scale on the B and E strings.

Example 3n

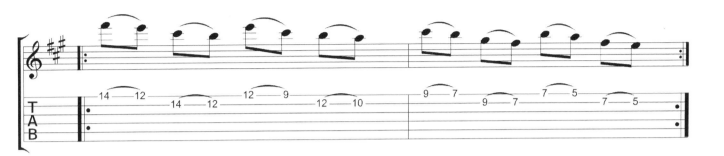

Bursts of Speed

One way to increase your endurance on the guitar is to introduce sudden bursts of speed into your practice regime. The next two examples use use 1/4 notes and 1/16th notes to show how to add an injection of pace into your workout.

The more you add bursts of speed to your finger-gym workouts, the longer you will be able to play at quicker speeds, and the easier it will be play at slower tempos.

Example 3o uses three 1/4 notes followed by four 1/16th notes throughout the entire A Major scale both ascending and descending. Make sure you pick a tempo that you can comfortably play 1/16th notes.

Example 3o

Example 3p, adds the speed burst at the start of each pattern instead of the end. This time four 1/16th notes proceed three 1/4 notes. For extra practice, try placing the 1/16th notes at different positions in the bar.

Example 3p

Endurance Conclusion

Building solid technique should always include endurance exercises. They will ensure you can play for longer periods at your highest level without running out of energy. The addition of 'burst' practice will mean you can play faster licks and runs; something most guitarists crave!

Record your progress in a guitar journal. Write down the date, time, duration, metronome speed and examples played. Aim for regular technique practice of 5 - 10 minutes a day, rather than a block of 30 minutes once a week.

Chapter Four - Scale Sequences

This chapter focuses on how to combine dexterity, strength and endurance by building scale sequences. I call the following exercises 'ultimate lick builders'.

The following examples use the A Major scale, but you should apply these ideas to other keys. As an alternative to using a metronome, try playing these melodic sequences along to Backing Track One.

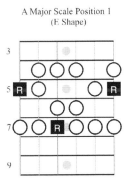

A Major Scale Position 1
(E Shape)

An effective way to practice scales is to combine groups of notes into patterns of threes or fours.

Example 4a – Three-note groupings ascending

Example 4b – Three-note groupings descending

Example 4c – Four-note groupings ascending

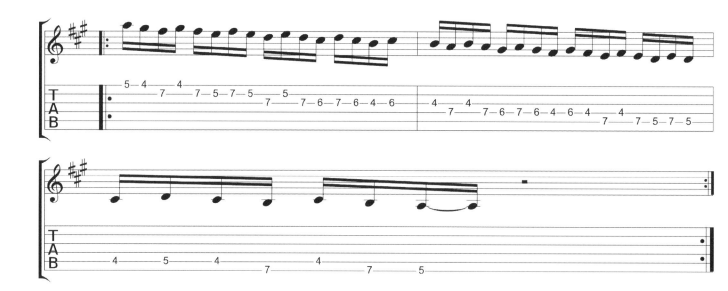

Example 4d – Four-note groupings descending

To melodic jumps to our melodies we can use interval skips. By using bigger intervals in solos, we can create exciting ideas that break away from predictable, linear scale runs.

In example 4e, we break the Major scale into intervals of a *3rd*.

Example 4e –3rds

In example 4e, the A Major scale is broken up into intervals of a 4th.

Example 4f – 4ths

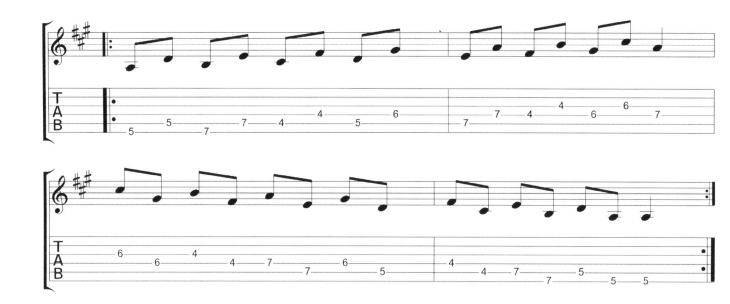

The next example uses the interval of a *5th*.

Example 4g – 5ths

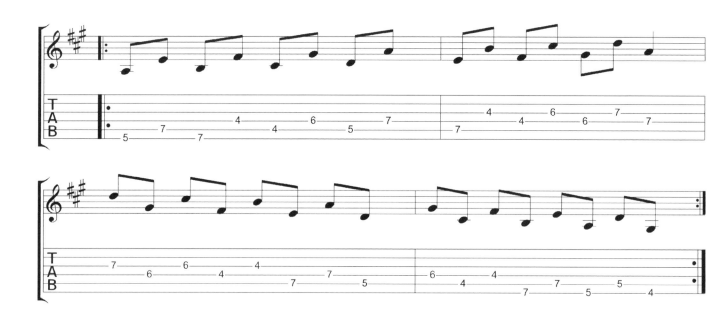

In example 4h, the A Major scale is played in *6ths*.

Example 4h – 6ths

Example 4i breaks up the A Major scale using the interval of a *7th*.

Example 4i – 7ths

The final interval jump, uses the A Major scale in octaves.

Example 4j – Octaves

Another way to add interest to your licks is to skip strings when playing scale shapes. In the next two examples, you can see how to create big melodic leaps by introducing string skips.

Example 4k – String Skipping ascending

Example 4l – String Skipping descending

An interesting way to practice scale sequences is to combine scale types within one exercise. In example 4m I have combined the C Major Pentatonic scale and the C Major scale into a two bar idea. Backing Track Two in C Major will work well with this example.

Example 4m – Major Pentatonic / Major scale

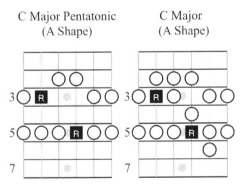

C Major Pentatonic
(A Shape)

C Major
(A Shape)

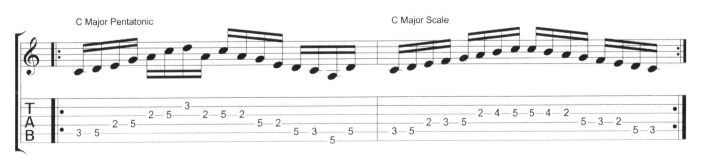

C Major Pentatonic

C Major Scale

Example 4n links the C Minor Pentatonic scale and the C Blues scale. This example works well with Backing Track Three in C minor.

Example 4n – Minor Pentatonic / Blues scale

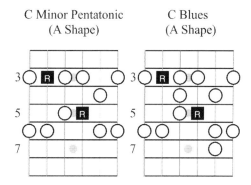

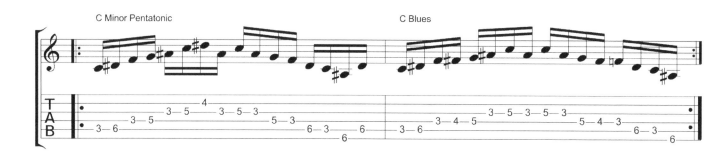

Example 4o blends the C Blues scale and the C Mixolydian scale into a useful sequence. Backing Track Four is in the key of C7 and works well underneath this example.

Example 4o –Blues scale / Mixolydian

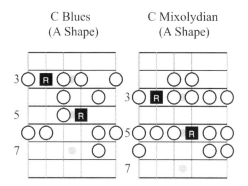

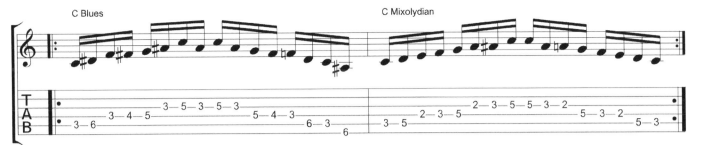

Refer to the appendix at the end of the book for full neck diagrams of common scale shapes.

For more scales patterns check out **Fretboard Fluency by Joseph Alexander.**

Chapter Five – Arpeggios and Chords

Another helpful way to train the fingers is to use arpeggios, and complex four-finger chord changes. In this chapter, I am going to show you how to build patterns and sequences around arpeggios and chord shapes to extend your dexterity in a highly musical context.

Arpeggios

'If you are worried or in doubt, always whip your arpeggio out.' Guitar Institute teacher, Max Milligan gave me this incredible advice and I will never forget it. In this chapter, you will learn how to build patterns and sequences using the A Major 7th (AMaj7), A Minor 7 (Am7) and A Dominant 7 (A7) arpeggios. For more arpeggio shapes refer to the appendix at the end of the book.

The first few examples use this AMaj7 arpeggio shape:

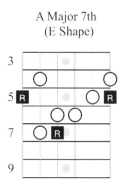

Example 5a ascends and descends the AMaj7 arpeggio in the E shape. Make sure that you apply strict alternate picking (down, up) and use the one-finger-per-fret system in each of the following examples.

Example 5a – AMaj7 Arpeggio

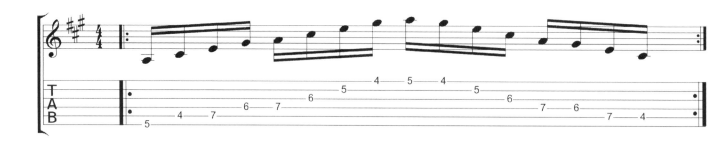

Example 5b descends through the AMaj7 arpeggio shape before ascending back up from the low root note A.

Example 5b – AMaj7 Arpeggio Reversed

Instead of playing the AMaj7 arpeggio shape sequentially, example 5c creates a 'Skip-a-Note' pattern. Be sure to try out all the AMaj7 arpeggios over Backing Track One.

Example 5c – AMaj7 Skip-a-Note

Another way to add interest to your arpeggios is to add string skips. Examples 5d and 5e sound more musical and exciting than just playing the arpeggio note by note.

Example 5d – AMaj7 String Skip Ascending

Example 5e – AMaj7 String Skip Descending

Now that you have mastered the AMaj7 arpeggio and useful variations, it is time to learn the A Minor 7 (Am7) arpeggio shape.

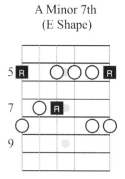

A Minor 7th
(E Shape)

Example 5f ascends and descends the Am7 arpeggio in the E shape.

Example 5f – Am7 Arpeggio

Descend the Am7 arpeggio from the high A note, before climbing back sequentially through the shape.

Example 5g – Am7 Arpeggio Reversed

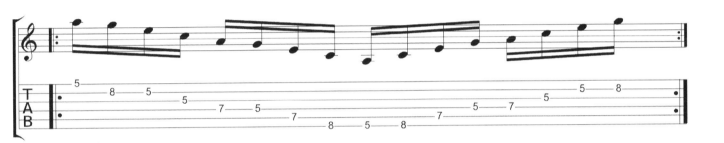

Example 5h creates a 'Skip-a-Note' pattern using the Am7 arpeggio in the E shape.

Example 5h – Am7 Skip-a-Note

Example 5i adds string skips to the Am7 arpeggio shape.

Example 5i – Am7 String Skip

The final arpeggio exercises use the A Dominant 7 (A7) arpeggio shape.

A Dominant 7th
(E Shape)

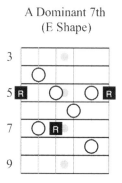

Example 5j ascends and descends the A7 arpeggio in the E shape.

Example 5j – A7 Arpeggio

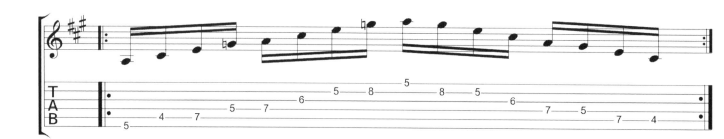

By starting at the high A note, example 5k creates a usable A7 arpeggio sequence.

Example 5k – A7 Arpeggio Reversed

Using 'Skip-a-Note' patterns helps you to break out of any arpeggio ruts.

Example 5l – A7 Skip-a-Note

The final arpeggio exercise in this chapter uses string skips to add excitement to the A Dominant 7 arpeggio.

Example 5m – A7 String Skip

Chords

Four-finger chord shapes are always a challenge and make a great addition to any finger-gym workout.

This example shows an AMaj7 to AMaj9 chord change, which requires every finger to move independently. This chord sequence is very common in jazz and Latin, making it both a practical warm up, and a useful rhythm playing fragment.

Example 5n – Amaj7 to Amaj9

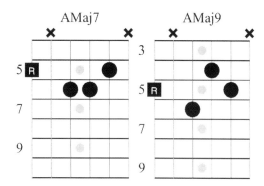

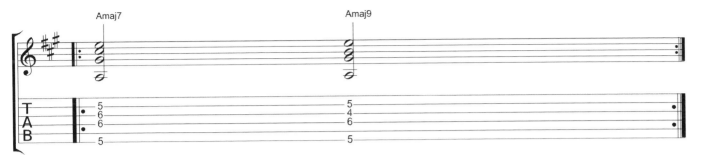

Example 5o uses a DMaj7 to DMaj9 chord sequence with the root notes on the A string. In this example your first finger will play the root note of D in the DMaj7 chord, but you will need to change it to your second finger when playing the DMaj9 chord.

Example 5o – DMaj7 to DMaj9

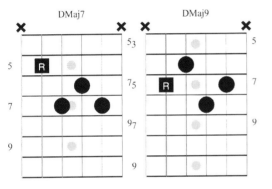

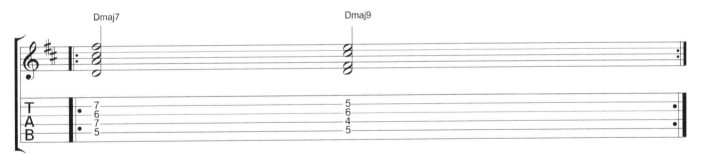

Example 5p uses another four-finger chord change, this time from Dm7 to Dm9.

Example 5p – Dm7 to Dm9

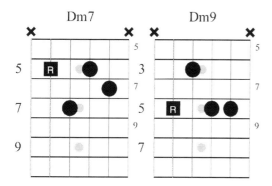

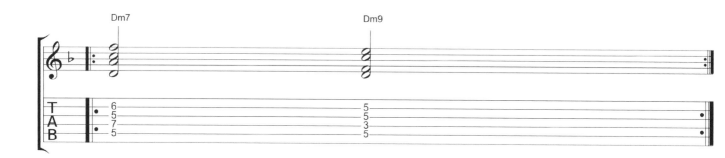

The final four-finger chord change is a D7 to D9 change with the root notes located on the A string.

The four-finger chord sequences shown throughout this chapter will not only provide an effective workout tool but can also act as useful rhythm playing licks.

Example 5q – D7 to D9

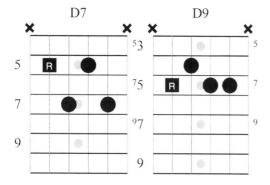

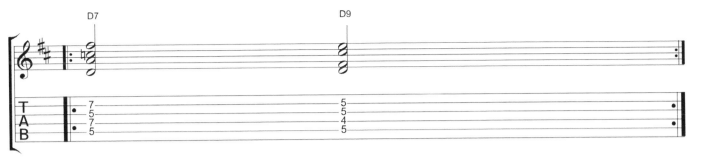

Arpeggios and Chords Conclusion

Scales, arpeggios, and chords provide the musical foundation for guitar playing. By building finger workouts around these common musical principles you can improve dexterity, coordination, stamina and strength in a melodic context. As with all the exercises in this book, you can work either through a whole chapter or practice an individual exercise until it feels comfortable. For example, I use example 5n daily as part of my finger-gym warm up regime.

Once you have completed the examples shown in this chapter, I urge you to play them in as many different keys as possible.

Chapter Six – Dexterous Driver

I have written a short piece of music that includes the main topics covered throughout this book. Dexterous driver has a neo-classical sound and will improve dexterity, coordination, and stamina. The piece is set around the A Harmonic Minor scale (A B C D E F G#) and the full neck diagram for this scale is shown below.

I recommend using strict alternate picking throughout this piece, but for an extra challenge, you can add hammer-ons and pull-offs to each four-note pattern once you have learnt the complete piece.

The fingering I use for the track is written above the notes. By following the suggested fingering pattern, you will ensure that each finger develops equally. Finish each workout by playing through Dexterous Driver.

Before attempting to play Dexterous Driver, listen to the audio track at least three times and then use the slow version of the recording to help you copy each bar individually. This way you will capture every nuance and master the correct phrasing.

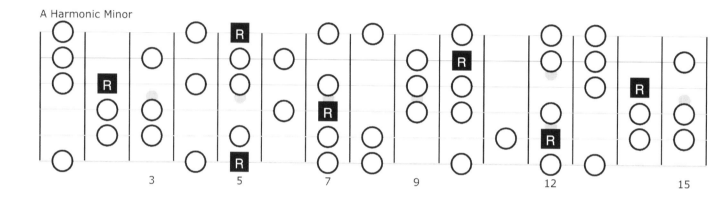

Example 6a Dexterous Driver

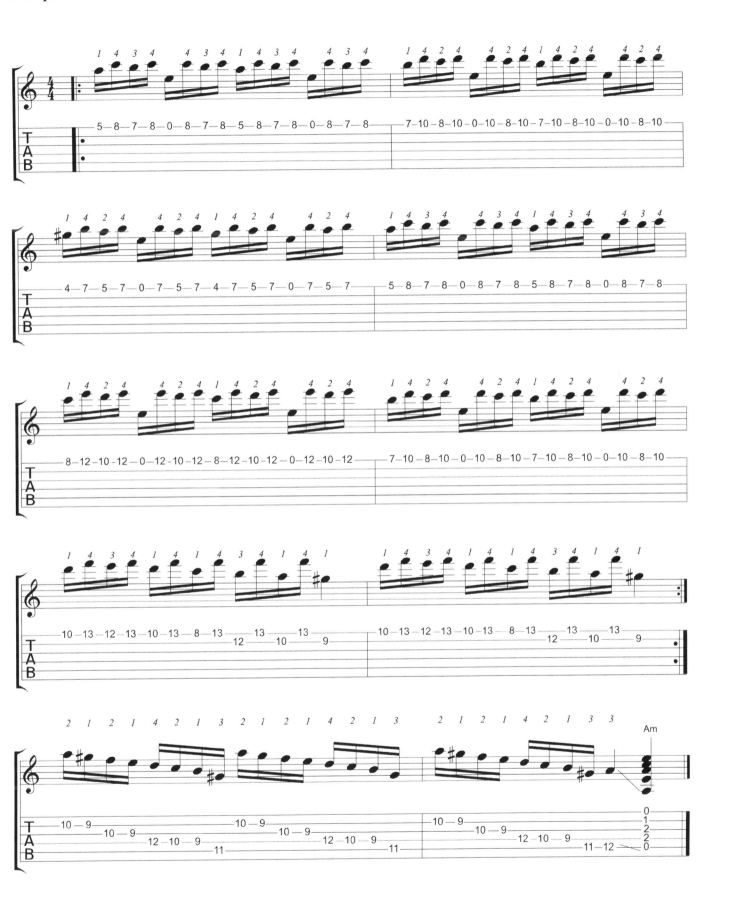

Once you have mastered this piece, learn the following song sections and add them to the end of your finger-gym workouts. They will make the process of mastering your guitar technique far more enjoyable as you will always be working towards a fun musical conclusion.

AC/DC – Thunderstruck (Intro riff)

Ozzy Osbourne – Crazy Train (Intro Riff)

Red Hot Chili Peppers – Snow (Main Riff)

The Killers – Mr Brightside (Main Riff)

Fleetwood Mac – Oh Well (Main Riff)

Rodrigo Y Gabriela – Hanuman

Jack Johnson – Belle

John Mayer – Queen Of California (Main Chord Riff)

The Beatles – Day Tripper (Main Riff)

Chapter Seven - Building The Perfect Workout

The perfect guitar finger-gym workout is one that fits around your individual needs, interests and ability. I have created a ten-minute, fifteen-minute, thirty-minute and one-hour workout suggestions for you below. These workouts are a guide, and can be customised in any way you wish. Each workout starts with example 1c and finishes with Dexterous Driver.

Use a metronome and a timer for each workout!

Sample 10 Minute Workout

Example Number	Number Of Reps	Metronome Speed	Total Time
1c	Constant for total time	60bpm (Increase Daily)	1 Minute
1d	Constant for total time	60bpm (Increase Daily)	1 Minute
1k	Constant for total time	60bpm (Increase Daily)	1 Minute
2g	Constant for total time	60bpm (Increase Daily)	1 Minute
2n	Constant for total time	60bpm (Increase Daily)	1 Minute
3o	Constant for total time	60bpm (Increase Daily)	1 Minute
4a	Constant for total time	60bpm (Increase Daily)	1 Minute
5h	Constant for total time	60bpm (Increase Daily)	1 Minute
6a	Constant for total time	60bpm (Increase Daily)	2 Minutes
			10 Minutes

Sample 15 Minute Workout

Example Number	Number Of Reps	Metronome Speed	Total Time
1c	Constant for total time	60bpm (Increase Daily)	1 Minute
1e	Constant for total time	60bpm (Increase Daily)	1 Minute
1h	Constant for total time	60bpm (Increase Daily)	1 Minute
2o	Constant for total time	60bpm (Increase Daily)	1 Minute
2p	Constant for total time	60bpm (Increase Daily)	1 Minute
2q	Constant for total time	60bpm (Increase Daily)	1 Minute
3b	Constant for total time	60bpm (Increase Daily)	1 Minute
3h	Constant for total time	60bpm (Increase Daily)	1 Minute
4f	Constant for total time	60bpm (Increase Daily)	1 Minute
5l	Constant for total time	60bpm (Increase Daily)	1 Minute
6a	Constant for total time	60bpm (Increase Daily)	5 Minutes
			15 Minutes

Sample 30 Minute Workout

You now spend longer on each example, giving you more time to practice any patterns or sequences you find challenging.

Example Number	Number Of Reps	Metronome Speed	Total Time
1c	Constant for total time	60bpm (Increase Daily)	2 Minutes
1f	Constant for total time	60bpm (Increase Daily)	2 Minutes
1g	Constant for total time	60bpm (Increase Daily)	2 Minutes
1j	Constant for total time	60bpm (Increase Daily)	2 Minutes
2g	Constant for total time	60bpm (Increase Daily)	2 Minutes
2n	Constant for total time	60bpm (Increase Daily)	2 Minutes
3m	Constant for total time	60bpm (Increase Daily)	2 Minutes
3n	Constant for total time	60bpm (Increase Daily)	2 Minutes
4g	Constant for total time	60bpm (Increase Daily)	2 Minutes
5h	Constant for total time	60bpm (Increase Daily)	2 Minutes
5n	Constant for total time	60bpm (Increase Daily)	2 Minutes
6a	Constant for total time	60bpm (Increase Daily)	8 Minutes
			30 Minutes

Sample 60 Minute Workout

Example Number	Number Of Reps	Metronome Speed	Total Time
1c	Constant for total time	60bpm (Increase Daily)	3 Minutes
1d	Constant for total time	60bpm (Increase Daily)	3 Minutes
1e	Constant for total time	60bpm (Increase Daily)	3 Minutes
1j	Constant for total time	60bpm (Increase Daily)	3 Minutes
1k	Constant for total time	60bpm (Increase Daily)	3 Minutes
2g	Constant for total time	60bpm (Increase Daily)	3 Minutes
2n	Constant for total time	60bpm (Increase Daily)	3 Minutes
3h	Constant for total time	60bpm (Increase Daily)	3 Minutes
3p	Constant for total time	60bpm (Increase Daily)	3 Minutes
4c	Constant for total time	60bpm (Increase Daily)	3 Minutes
4d	Constant for total time	60bpm (Increase Daily)	3 Minutes
4j	Constant for total time	60bpm (Increase Daily)	3 Minutes
5e	Constant for total time	60bpm (Increase Daily)	3 Minutes
5i	Constant for total time	60bpm (Increase Daily)	3 Minutes
5m	Constant for total time	60bpm (Increase Daily)	3 Minutes
6a	Constant for total time	60bpm (Increase Daily)	15 Minutes
			60 Minutes

Further Study

This 'FundEssential' mini-book has been a focused look at how to build strength, stamina and coordination in all your fingers, but we also publish many full-length guides to playing the guitar. Each book is over 100 pages and includes hundreds of audio examples that you can download for free.

We've sold over 120,000 books on Amazon and are the highest rated, most popular guitar books available. The following is a selection of our most popular titles. Click the images for more information or go to

www.fundamental-changes.com/book for more information and over *250 free lessons and resources*.

My passion in life is teaching people to play and express themselves through the guitar. If you have any questions, please get in touch and I will do my best to respond as quickly as possible.

You can contact me on simeypratt@gmail.com or via the Fundamental Changes YouTube channel.

Appendix – Common Scale and Arpeggio Shapes

Earlier in this book I have referenced additional scales and arpeggios. The following appendix includes some of the most common scale shapes and arpeggios that you can use in your future finger-gym workouts. All of the following scales and arpeggios have a root note of C.

These scales are in order of my personal teaching preference, however, you can learn them in any order you wish. You can apply any of the patterns and sequences seen throughout this book to any of these scale and arpeggio shapes.

Common Scale Shapes

C Minor Pentatonic – 'C Eb F G Bb' (1 b3 4 5 b7) – Use with C minor.

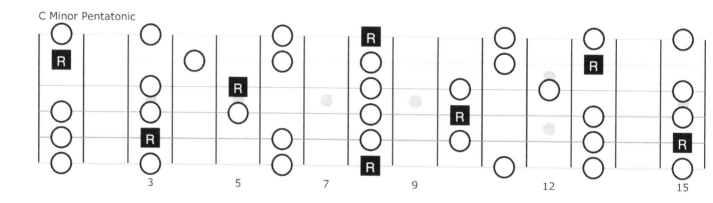

C Blues – 'C Eb F Gb G Bb' (1 b3 4 b5 5 b7) – Use with C minor or C7.

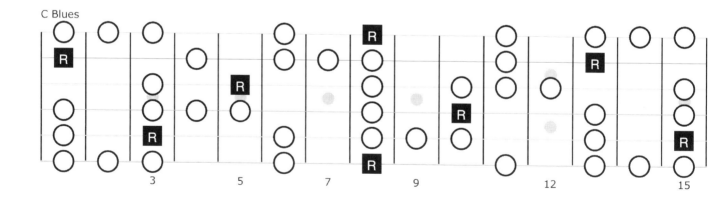

C Major Pentatonic – 'C D E G A' (1 2 3 5 6) – Use with C Major.

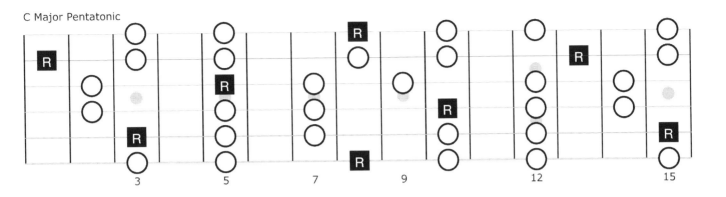

C Major Pentatonic

C Major Scale – 'C D E F G A B' (1 2 3 4 5 6 7) – Use with C Major.

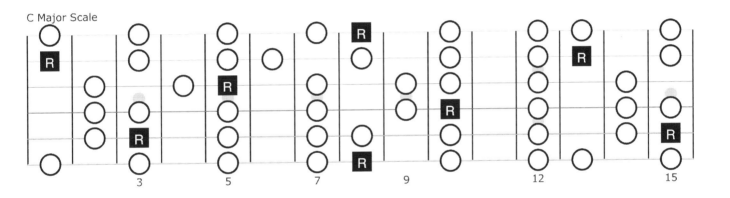

C Major Scale

C Natural Minor (Aeolian) Scale – 'C D Eb F G Ab Bb' (1 2 b3 4 5 b6 b7) – Use with C minor.

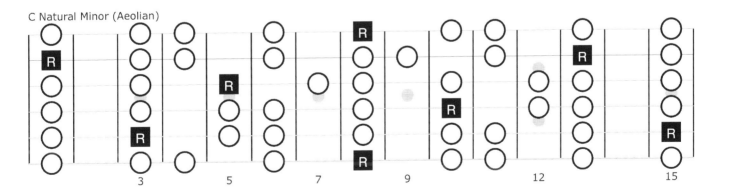

C Natural Minor (Aeolian)

C Mixolydian Scale – 'C D E F G A Bb' (1 2 3 4 5 6 b7) – Use with C7.

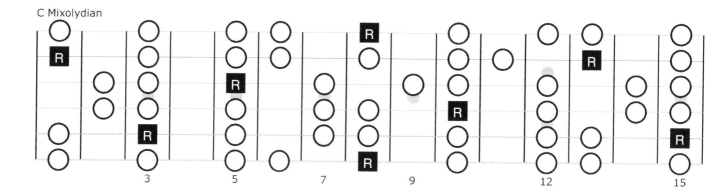

C Dorian Scale – 'C D Eb F G A Bb' (1 2 b3 4 5 6 b7) – Use with C minor.

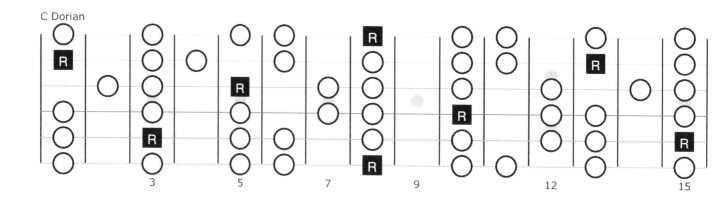

C Lydian Scale – 'C D E F# G A B' (1 2 3 #4 5 6 7) – Use with Cmaj7#11.

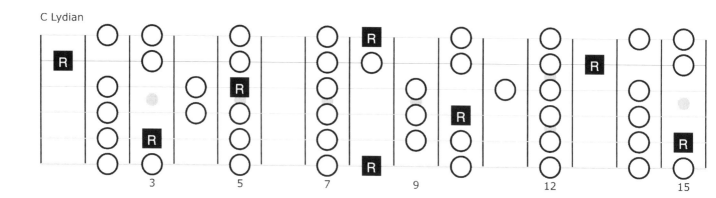

C Phrygian Scale – 'C Db Eb F G Ab Bb' (1 b2 b3 4 5 b6 b7) – Use with C Minor.

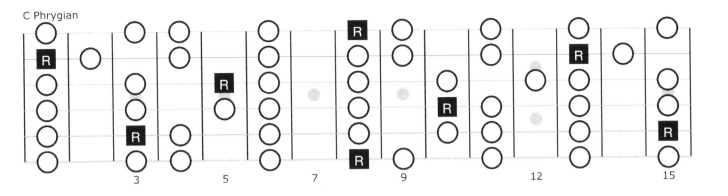

C Locrian Scale – 'C Db Eb F Gb Ab Bb' (1 b2 b3 4 b5 b6 b7) – Use with C Minor.

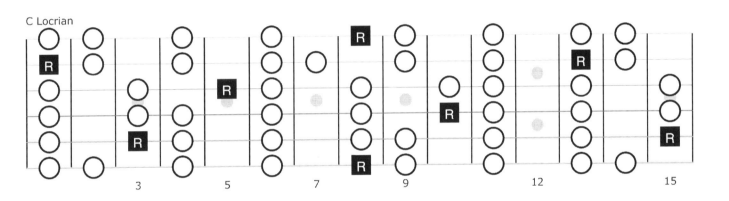

C Harmonic Minor Scale – 'C D Eb F G Ab B' (1 2 b3 4 5 b6 7) – Use with C Minor.

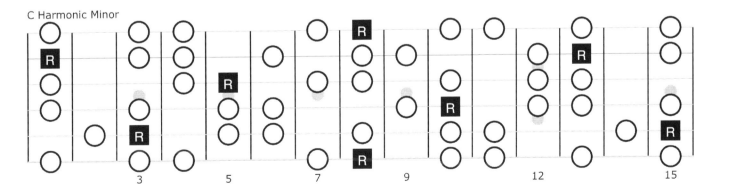

C Melodic Minor Scale – 'C D Eb F G A B' (1 2 b3 4 5 6 7) – Use with CmMaj7.

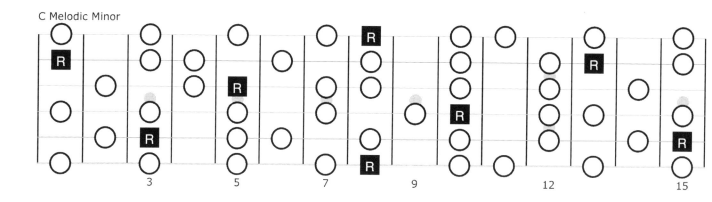

C Altered (Superlocrian) Scale 'C Db Eb E Gb Ab Bb' (1 b2 b3 bb4 b5 b6 b7) – Use with altered Dominant chords (7b5, 7#5, 7b9, 7#9 etc).

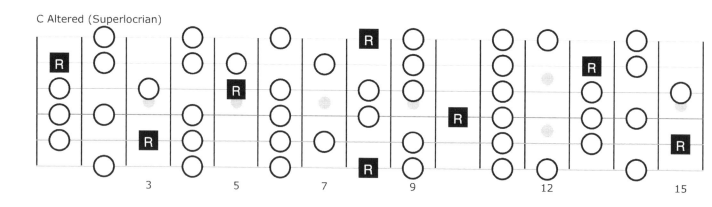

C Phyrgian Dominant Scale - 'C Db E F G Ab Bb' (1 b2 3 4 5 b6 b7) – Use with C minor.

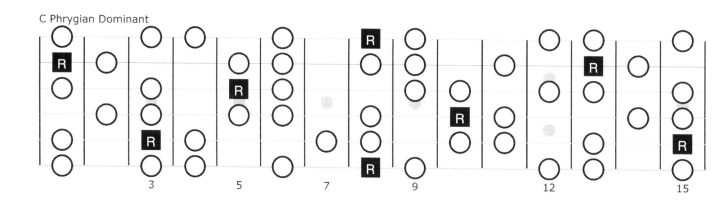

C Lydian Dominant Scale – 'C D E F# G A Bb' (1 2 3 #4 5 6 b7) – Use with 7#11 chords.

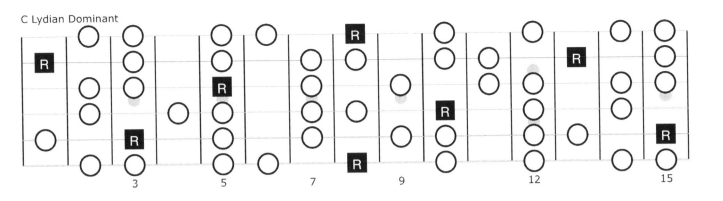

C Half-Whole Scale – 'C Db D# E F# G A Bb' (1 b2 #2 3 #4 5 6 b7) – Use with 13b9 chords.

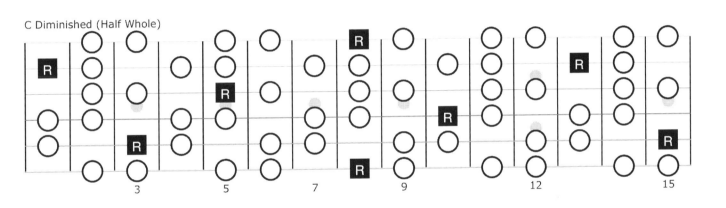

C Whole Tone Scale – ' C D Eb F Gb G# A B' (1 2 b3 4 b5 #5 6 7) – Use with dim7 and 7b9 chords.

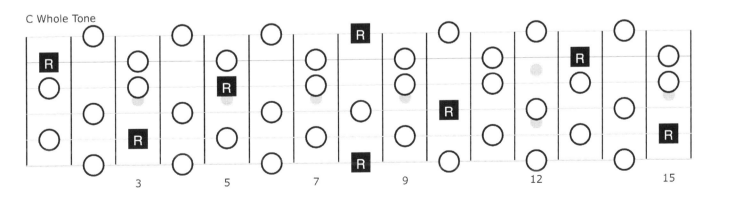

Common Triad and Arpeggio Shapes

I have also included some common arpeggio to build into your finger-gym workouts with the patterns and sequences seen throughout this book. I have included the five CAGED shapes and a full neck diagram for each arpeggio shape. For more information on the CAGED system check out my book Exotic Pentatonic Soloing For Guitar.

C Major Triad Arpeggio – 'C E G' (1 3 5) – Use with C Major chords.

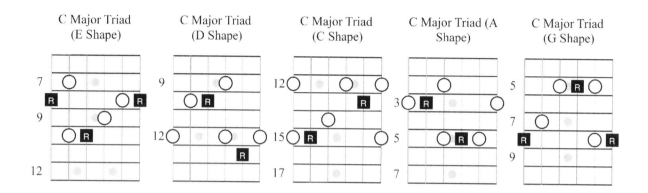

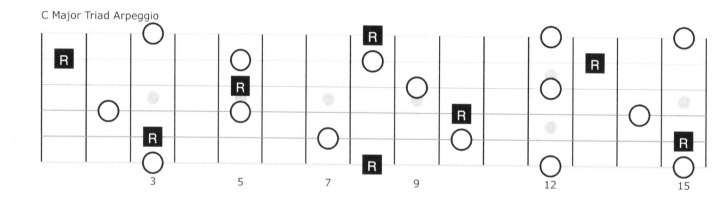

C Minor Triad Arpeggio – 'C Eb G' (1 b3 5) – Use with C minor chords.

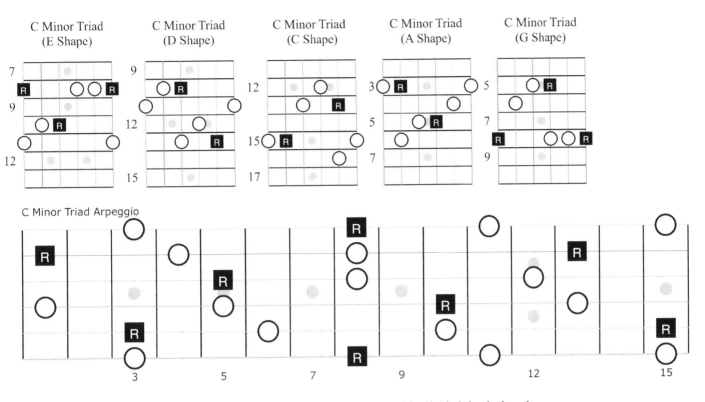

C Diminished Triad Arpeggio – 'C Eb Gb' (1 b3 b5) – Use with diminished chords.

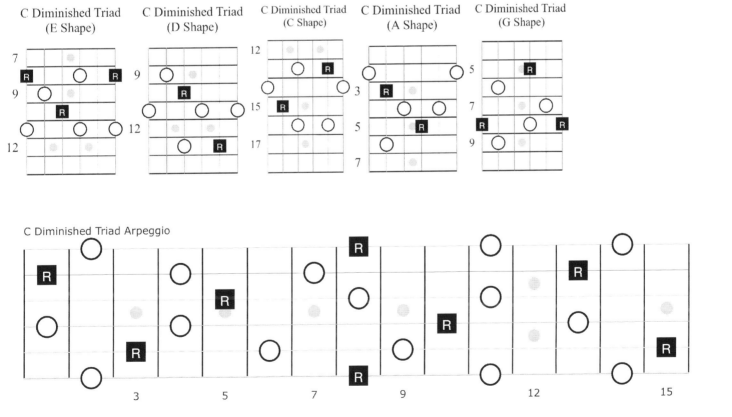

C Augmented Triad Arpeggio – 'C E G#' (1 3 #5) – Use with augmented chords

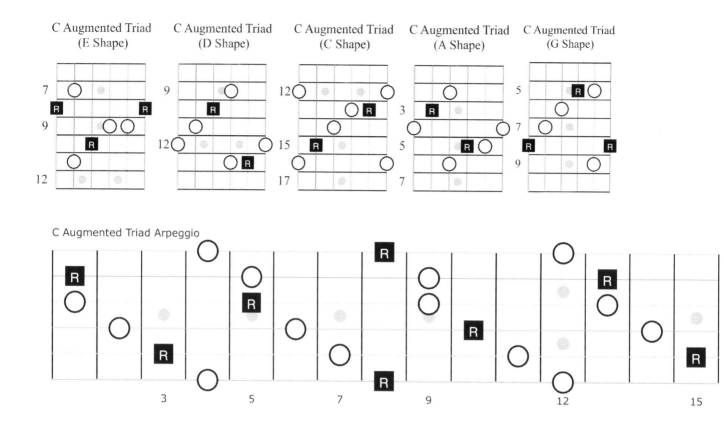

C Major 7th Arpeggio – 'C E G B' (1 3 5 7) – Use with C Major 7th chords

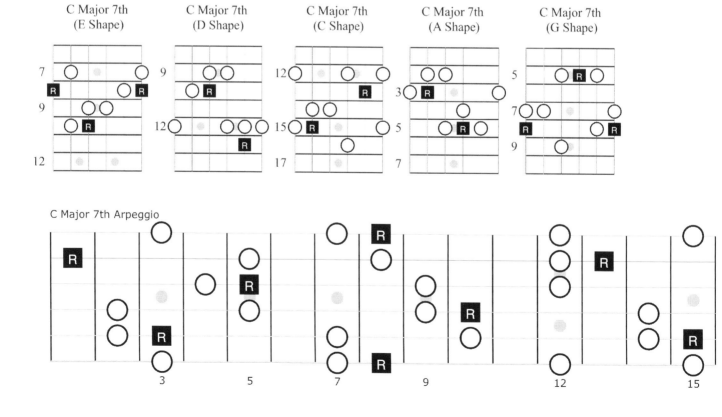

C Minor 7 Arpeggio - 'C Eb G Bb' (1 b3 5 b7) – Use with C Minor 7 chords

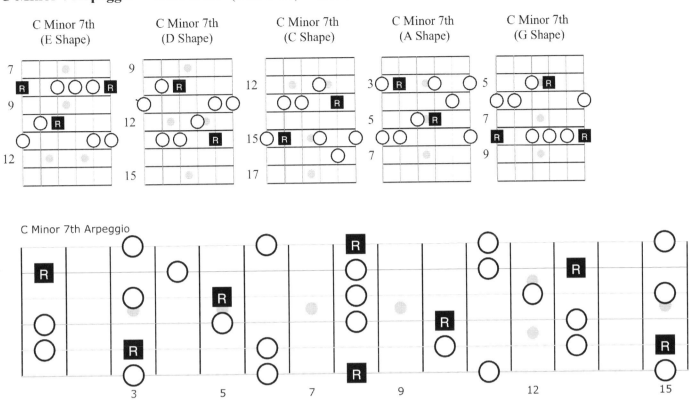

C Minor 7th (E Shape)   C Minor 7th (D Shape)   C Minor 7th (C Shape)   C Minor 7th (A Shape)   C Minor 7th (G Shape)

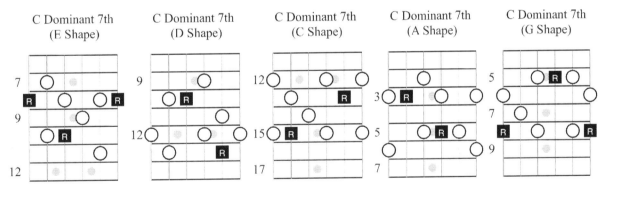

C Minor 7th Arpeggio

C Dominant 7 Arpeggio - 'C E G Bb' (1 3 5 b7) – Use with C Dominant 7 chords

C Dominant 7th (E Shape)   C Dominant 7th (D Shape)   C Dominant 7th (C Shape)   C Dominant 7th (A Shape)   C Dominant 7th (G Shape)

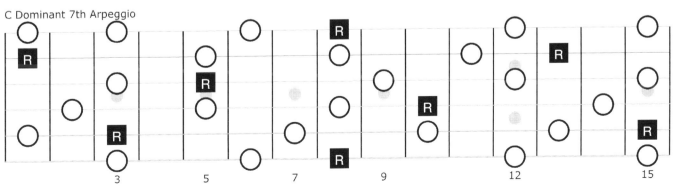

C Dominant 7th Arpeggio

C Minor 7b5 Arpeggio - 'C Eb Gb Bb' (R b3 b5 b7) – Use with C minor 7b5 chords

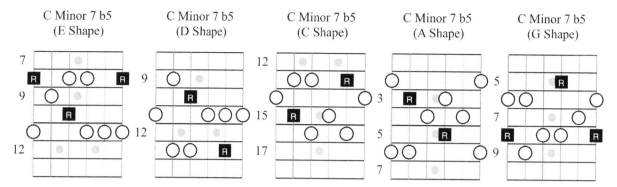

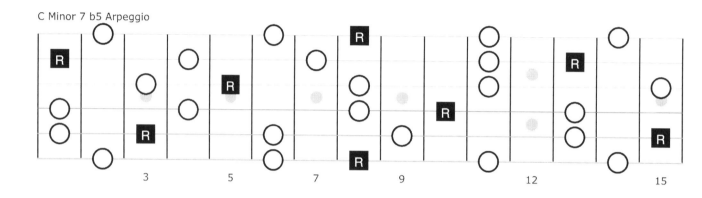

Other Books from Fundamental Changes

The Complete Guide to Playing Blues Guitar Book One: Rhythm Guitar

The Complete Guide to Playing Blues Guitar Book Two: Melodic Phrasing

The Complete Guide to Playing Blues Guitar Book Three: Beyond Pentatonics

The Complete Guide to Playing Blues Guitar Compilation

The CAGED System and 100 Licks for Blues Guitar

Minor ii V Mastery for Jazz Guitar

Jazz Blues Soloing for Guitar

Guitar Scales in Context

Guitar Chords in Context

The First 100 Chords for Guitar

Jazz Guitar Chord Mastery

Complete Technique for Modern Guitar

Funk Guitar Mastery

The Complete Technique, Theory & Scales Compilation for Guitar

Sight Reading Mastery for Guitar

Rock Guitar Un-CAGED

The Practical Guide to Modern Music Theory for Guitarists

Beginner's Guitar Lessons: The Essential Guide

Chord Tone Soloing for Jazz Guitar

Chord Tone Soloing for Bass Guitar

Voice Leading Jazz Guitar

Guitar Fretboard Fluency

The Circle of Fifths for Guitarists

First Chord Progressions for Guitar

The First 100 Jazz Chords for Guitar

100 Country Licks for Guitar

Pop & Rock Ukulele Strumming

Walking Bass for Jazz and Blues

Guitar Finger Gym

The Melodic Minor Cookbook

The Chicago Blues Guitar Method

Heavy Metal Rhythm Guitar

Heavy Metal Lead Guitar

Progressive Metal Guitar

Heavy Metal Guitar Bible

Exotic Pentatonic Soloing for Guitar

The Complete Jazz Guitar Soloing Compilation

The Jazz Guitar Chords Compilation

Fingerstyle Blues Guitar

The Complete DADGAD Guitar Method

Country Guitar for Beginners

Beginner Lead Guitar Method

The Country Fingerstyle Guitar Method

Beyond Rhythm Guitar

Rock Rhythm Guitar Playing

Fundamental Changes in Jazz Guitar

Neo-Classical Speed Strategies for Guitar

100 Classic Rock Licks for Guitar

The Beginner's Guitar Method Compilation

100 Classic Blues Licks for Guitar

The Country Guitar Method Compilation

Country Guitar Soloing Techniques

Printed by Amazon Italia Logistica S.r.l.
Torrazza Piemonte (TO), Italy

15601607R00039